Kids'
KOOKIEST
Knock-Knocks

Jacqueline Horsfall

Illustrated by
Tamara Petrosino

Sterling Publishing Co., Inc.
New York

For Nonna and Jean

Library of Congress Cataloging-in-Publication Data

Horsfall, Jacqueline.
 Kids' kookiest knock-knocks / Jacqueline Horsfall; illustrated by Tamara Petrosino.
  p. cm.
 Includes index.
 ISBN-13: 978-1-4027-1741-3
 ISBN-10: 1-4027-1741-5
1. Knock-knock jokes. I. Petrosino, Tamara. II. Title.
PN6231.K55H65 2006
818'.602--dc22

                          2006017312

10 9 8 7 6 5 4 3 2 1

Published by Sterling Publishing Co., Inc.
387 Park Avenue South, New York, NY 10016
Text © 2006 by Jacqueline Horsfall
Illustrations © 2006 by Tamara Petrosino
Distributed in Canada by Sterling Publishing
℅ Canadian Manda Group, 165 Dufferin Street
Toronto, Ontario, Canada M6K 3H6
Distributed in the United Kingdom by GMC Distribution Services
Castle Place, 166 High Street, Lewes, East Sussex, England BN7 1XU
Distributed in Australia by Capricorn Link (Australia) Pty. Ltd.
P.O. Box 704, Windsor, NSW 2756, Australia

Manufactured in the United States of America
All rights reserved

Sterling ISBN-13: 978-1-4027-1741-3
        ISBN-10: 1-4027-1741-5

For information about custom editions, special sales, premium and
corporate purchases, please contact Sterling Special Sales
Department at 800-805-5489 or specialsales@sterlingpub.com.

Knock-knock.
  Who's there?
Adele.
    Adele who?
Adele is what the farmer stands in.

  Knock-knock.
    Who's there?
  Al dente.
      Al dente who?
  Al dente my fender!

Knock-knock.
  Who's there?
Al E.
    Al E. who?
Al E. cats meowing at
your door.

Knock-knock.
  Who's there?
Albie.
  Albie who?
Albie there as soon as I
scrape this gum off my shoe.

Knock-knock.
  Who's there?
Alma.
  Alma who?
Alma underwear is in
the dryer!

Knock-knock.
  Who's there?
Alpaca.
  Alpaca who?
Alpaca picnic for us.

Knock-knock.
  Who's there?
Amish.
  Amish who?
Amish you a whole lot.

Knock-knock.
  Who's there?
Annette.
  Annette who?
Annette is all you need to catch
butterflies.

Knock-knock.
  Who's there?
Annie.
  Annie who?
Annie reason this door's locked?

Knock-knock.
  Who's there?
Anteater.
  Anteater who?
Anteater pizza and uncle
eater crusts.

Knock-knock.
  Who's there?
Arthur.
  Arthur who?
Arthur any cookies left?

5

Knock-knock.
   Who's there?
Artie.
   Artie who?
Artie chokes are healthy
vegetables.

Knock-knock.
   Who's there?
Astor.
   Astor who?
Astor a question, but she
wouldn't answer me.

Knock-knock.
   Who's there?
Athena.
   Athena who?
Athena U.F.O.
last night.

Knock-knock.
   Who's there?
August.
   August who?
August of wind blew my
homework away . . . honest!

Knock-knock.
   Who's there?
Avenue.
   Avenue who?
Avenue heard enough knock-
knocks for now?

Knock-knock.
Who's there?
Baby blue.
Baby blue who?
Baby blue bubbles in the bath water.

Knock-knock.
Who's there?
Baby owl.
Baby owl who?
Baby owl always love you.

Knock-knock.
Who's there?
Bach.
Bach who?
Bach door's open, so I
came in that way.

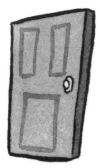

Knock-knock.
Who's there?
Bah.
Bah who?
Bah-loney sandwich!

Knock-knock.
Who's there?
Bean.
Bean who?
Bean only a kid,
I can't drive yet.

Knock-knock.
Who's there?
Becka.
Becka who?
Becka the bus is the best
place to sit.

Knock-knock.
Who's there?
Beef or veal.
Beef or veal who?
Beef or you go, veal you please eat your dinner?

Knock-knock.
 Who's there?
Beets and carrot.
 Beets and carrot who?
Beets me who'll win the game—
really don't carrot all.

Knock-knock.
 Who's there?
Bella.
 Bella who?
Bella stuck, so I knocked.

Knock-knock.
 Who's there?
Berry.
 Berry who?
Berry pleased to meet you.

Knock-knock.
 Who's there?
Bette.
 Bette who?
Bette you can't catch me.

Knock-knock.
 Who's there?
Blah, blah.
 Blah, blah who?
Blah, blah black sheep,
have you any wool?

9

Knock-knock.
   Who's there?
Brandon.
   Brandon who?
Brandon steers is what cowhands do on a ranch.

Knock-knock.
   Who's there?
Buccaneer.
   Buccaneer who?
Buccaneer sounds like an awful lot to pay for corn.

Knock-knock.
   Who's there?
Bugs.
   Bugs who?
Bugs me when you keep asking who's there.

Knock-knock.
   Who's there?
Bugspray.
   Bugspray who?
Bugspray that bats won't eat them.

Knock-knock.
   Who's there?
Buster.
   Buster who?
Buster dollhouse up and your baby sister will cry.

Knock-knock.
   Who's there?
Butcher.
   Butcher who?
Butcher arms around me, Honey.

Knock-knock.
   Who's there?
Butternut.
   Butternut who?
Butternut come any closer.

Knock-knock.
   Who's there?
Button.
   Button who?
Button in line isn't very polite.

Knock-knock.
　　Who's there?
Canal.
　　Canal who?
Canal come out and play?

Knock-knock.
　　Who's there?
Candy.
　　Candy who?
Candy other kids come out
and play if Al can't?

Knock-knock.
   Who's there?
Cara.
   Cara who?
Cara lot about you, Honey.

Knock-knock.
   Who's there?
Carey.
   Carey who?
Carey me in! I've been
knocking all day!

Knock-knock.
   Who's there?
Cargo.
   Cargo who?
Cargo beep-beep.
Truck go vroom-vroom.

Knock-knock.
   Who's there?
Carl.
   Carl who?
Carl get you there
faster than a bus.

Knock-knock.
   Who's there?
Carmen.
   Carmen who?
Carmen get it! Dinner's
ready!

Knock-knock.
   Who's there?
Carrot and peas.
   Carrot and peas who?
Carrot all about world peas?

Knock-knock.
  Who's there?
Cash.
  Cash who?
Cashew? You're nuts!

Knock-knock.
  Who's there?
Cedar and poplar.
  Cedar and poplar who?
Cedar girl over there? She's
really poplar.

Knock-knock.
  Who's there?
Celia.
  Celia who?
Celia letters before
you mail them.

Knock-knock.
  Who's there?
Cereal.
  Cereal who?
Cereal pleasure to meet you.

Knock-knock.
  Who's there?
Charlotta.
  Charlotta who?
Charlotta fireflies out tonight.

Knock-knock.
  Who's there?
Cheese.
  Cheese who?
Cheese a real cute girl,
don't you think?

Knock-knock.
   Who's there?
Chili.
   Chili who?
Chili out here. Can I come in?

Knock-knock.
   Who's there?
Cindy.
   Cindy who?
Cindy DVD to my house after you've watched it.

Knock-knock.
  Who's there?
Claire.
  Claire who?
Claire nights are good for stargazing.

Knock-knock.
  Who's there?
Clarence.
  Clarence who?
Clarence sale! Half price!

Knock-knock.
  Who's there?
Closure.
  Closure who?
Closure mouth when you chew.

Knock-knock.
Who's there?
Clothesline.
Clothesline who?
Clothesline all over your
bedroom floor.

Knock-knock.
Who's there?
Colleen.
Colleen who?
Colleen socks, new jeans . . .
I'm ready for school.

Knock-knock.
Who's there?
Collin.
Collin who?
Collin you on your cell phone, but
you didn't answer.

Knock-knock.
Who's there?
Comma.
Comma who?
Comma way with me, my love.

Knock-knock.
Who's there?
Cuba.
Cuba who?
Cuba sugar for my tea, please.

Knock-knock.
Who's there?
Daisy.
Daisy who?
Daisy goes to
school, nights he
does homework.

Knock-knock.
Who's there?
Dale.
Dale who?
Dale dawn when the sun rises.

Knock-knock.
　Who's there?
Dancer.
　Dancer who?
Dancer is simple—it's me
knocking.

Knock-knock.
　Who's there?
Data.
　Data who?
Data good dog!

Knock-knock.
　Who's there?
Delight.
　Delight who?
Delight's on in de living room.

Knock-knock.
　Who's there?
Dennis.
　Dennis who?
Dennis where bears hibernate
in winter.

Knock-knock.
　Who's there?
Dionne.
　Dionne who?
Dionne switch is up; de off switch is down.

Knock-knock.
  Who's there?
Diploma.
  Diploma who?
Diploma fixed our leaky faucet.

Knock-knock.
  Who's there?
Disappears.
  Disappears who?
Disappears to be
de right house.

Knock-knock.
  Who's there?
Disease.
  Disease who?
Disease jeans fit me?

Knock-knock.
  Who's there?
Dogwood.
  Dogwood who?
Dogwood sure make a good pet.

Knock-knock.
  Who's there?
Doris.
  Doris who?
Doris locked—open up!

Knock-knock.
  Who's there?
Doughnut.
  Doughnut who?
Doughnut tell anyone I
knocked.

Knock-knock.
  Who's there?
Dozen.
  Dozen who?
Dozen your bell ever work?

Knock-knock.
  Who's there?
Dozen Olga.
  Dozen Olga who?
  You're right! An owl does go "who"!

Knock-knock.
  Who's there?
Dragon.
  Dragon who?
Dragon my suitcase—let me in!

E

Knock-knock.
    Who's there?
Ears and nose.
    Ears and nose who?
Ears a secret no one nose but you.

Knock-knock.
    Who's there?
E-mail.
    E-mail who?
E-mail; she female.

Knock-knock.
   Who's there?
Eartha.
   Eartha who?
Eartha bit farther from
the sun than Venus.

Knock-knock.
   Who's there?
Easter.
   Easter who?
   Easter west, home's best.

Knock-knock.
   Who's there?
Eda.
   Eda who?
Eda spider and you'll probably barf!

Knock-knock.
   Who's there?
Eerie.
   Eerie who?
Eerie comes, ready
or not!

Knock-knock.
   Who's there?
Edwina.
   Edwina who?
Edwina trip to Disney World!

Knock-knock.
   Who's there?
Eiffel.
   Eiffel who?
Eiffel down, can you help me up?

23

Knock-knock.
　Who's there?
Eileen.
　　Eileen who?
Eileen over to wash between
my toes.

Knock-knock.
　Who's there?
Elsie.
　　Elsie who?
Elsie you later!

Knock-knock.
　Who's there?
Emma.
　　Emma who?
Emma real expert when it comes to ice cream.

Knock-knock.
Who's there?
Enoch.
Enoch who?
Enoch and Enoch, but no
one answers the door.

Knock-knock.
Who's there?
Erskine.
Erskine who?
Erskine itches from so many
mosquito bites.

Knock-knock.
Who's there?
Esther.
Esther who?
Esther anything I can do for you?

Knock-knock.
Who's there?
Ether.
Ether who?
Ether bunny might
leave you some
jellybeans.

Knock-knock.
Who's there?
Etta.
Etta who?
Etta worm . . . now
I feel sick.

Knock-knock.
Who's there?
Europe.
Europe who?
Europe next, so please hit a home run.

Knock-knock.
    Who's there?
Evan.
    Evan who?
Evan is a place where angels live.

Knock-knock.
    Who's there?
Ewe.
    Ewe who?
Ewe and I make
a great couple.

Knock-knock.
    Who's there?
Eye color.
    Eye color who?
Eye color in my coloring book with my crayons.

Knock-knock.
  Who's there?
Fairy.
  Fairy who?
Fairy pleased to meet you.

Knock-knock.
  Who's there?
Falafel.
  Falafel who?
Falafel off her bike and
skinned her knee.

Knock-knock.
  Who's there?
Fangs.
  Fangs who?
Fangs a lot for inviting me over!

27

Knock-knock.
  Who's there?
Fanny.
  Fanny who?
Fanny body home?

Knock-knock.
  Who's there?
Ferdie.
  Ferdie who?
Ferdie last time, I did not borrow
your toothbrush!

Knock-knock.
  Who's there?
Figs.
  Figs who?
Figs your doorbell,
will you?

Knock-knock.
  Who's there?
Fillmore.
  Fillmore who?
Fillmore soda cups, please.

Knock-knock.
   Who's there?
Fish sticks.
   Fish sticks who?
Fish sticks to the frying
pan if you don't oil it first.

Knock-knock.
   Who's there?
Five.
   Five who?
Five really got to go . . . see you later!

Knock-knock.
   Who's there?
Fixture.
   Fixture who?
Fixture doorbell . . . ding-dong! Like it?

29

Knock-knock.
  Who's there?
Flora.
  Flora who?
Flora my room is
covered with dirty
clothes.

Knock-knock.
  Who's there?
Florida.
  Florida who?
Florida bathroom is soaking wet.

Knock-knock.
  Who's there?
Flossie.
  Flossie who?
Flossie your teeth everyday is a good habit!

Knock-knock.
Who's there?
Fonda.
Fonda who?
Fonda you, Sweetie.

Knock-knock.
Who's there?
Fortitude.
Fortitude who?
Fortitude plus one equals forty-three.

Knock-knock.
Who's there?
Foster.
Foster who?
Foster than a speeding bullet!

Knock-knock.
Who's there?
Francis.
Francis who?
Francis where people speak French.

Knock-knock.
Who's there?
Freddie.
Freddie who?
Freddie or not, I'm busting through this door!

Knock-knock.
Who's there?
Freezer.
Freezer who?
Freezer I'll call the cops!

Knock-knock.
   Who's there?
G. I.
   G. I. who?
G. I. really like you.

Knock-knock.
   Who's there?
Gamma.
   Gamma who?
Gamma and Gampa are my
favorite relatives.

Knock-knock.
   Who's there?
Garden.
   Garden who?
Garden the castle is a
knight's job.

Knock-knock.
   Who's there?
Gateway.
   Gateway who?
Gateway a ton—I can't
budge it!

Knock-knock.
   Who's there?
Geyser.
   Geyser who?
Geyser usually shy
around cute girls.

   Knock-knock.
      Who's there?
Gibson.
      Gibson who?
Gibson back—you took too much!

   Knock-knock.
      Who's there?
Gingersnaps.
      Gingersnaps who?
Gingersnaps her fingers, and
boys come running.

Knock-knock.
   Who's there?
Glasses.
   Glasses who?
Glasses what you pour your drink into.

   Knock-knock.
      Who's there?
Gnu.
      Gnu who?
Gnu you'd ask that . . . I don't have a clue.

33

Knock-knock.
  Who's there?
Gorillas go.
  Gorillas go who?
No, owls go who . . . gorillas go "AARRGH"!

Knock-knock.
  Who's there?
Grover.
  Grover who?
Grover there and get me
a cookie.

Knock-knock.
  Who's there?
Gum.
  Gum who?
Gum on out—let's play!

Knock-knock.
  Who's there?
Gustav.
  Gustav who?
Gustav wind blew my cap off!

Knock-knock.
  Who's there?
Gwyn.
  Gwyn who?
Gwyn fishing? Can
I come too?

Knock-knock.
  Who's there?
Half E.
  Half E who?
Half E birfday to you!

Knock-knock.
  Who's there?
Halo.
  Halo who?
Halo there! Anybody home?

Knock-knock.
  Who's there?
Hammond.
  Hammond who?
Hammond eggs are NOT a pig's favorite breakfast.

Knock-knock.
  Who's there?
Handsome.
  Handsome who?
Handsome raisins to me.

Knock-knock.
  Who's there?
Hari.
  Hari who?
Hari up or I'll leave without you

Knock-knock.
  Who's there?
Heaven.
  Heaven who?
Heaven you cleaned up your room yet?

Knock-knock.
  Who's there?
Hedda.
  Hedda who?
Hedda lettuce makes a
great salad.

Knock-knock.
  Who's there?
Heel.
    Heel who?
  Heel be here any
  minute now.

Knock-knock.
  Who's there?
Holden.
    Holden who?
  Holden hands with you, Darling.

Knock-knock.
  Who's there?
Hollywood.
  Hollywood who?
Hollywood play football if the coach
would let her join the team.

Knock-knock.
  Who's there?
House.
  House who?
House it going?

Knock-knock.
  Who's there?
Houseflies.
  Houseflies who?
Houseflies up in the air during a tornado.

37

Knock-knock.
   Who's there?
Howie.
   Howie who?
Howie going to get to school
if the bus doesn't come?

Knock-knock.
   Who's there?
Howl.
   Howl who?
Howl I eat this spaghetti
without a fork?

Knock-knock.
   Who's there?
Hugh.
   Hugh who?
Hugh going to open
up, or what?

Knock-knock.
   Who's there?
Hugo.
   Hugo who?
Hugo first, I'm too chicken

Knock-knock.
   Who's there?
Huron.
   Huron who?
Huron time, for once.

Knock-knock.
   Who's there?
I am.
   I am who?
Don't you even know
your own name?

Knock-knock.
   Who's there?
I love.
   I love who?
You love me, don't you?

Knock-knock.
   Who's there?
I. M.
   I. M. who?
I. M. the monster . . .
arrggh!

39

Knock-knock.
   Who's there?
Ice cream soda.
   Ice cream soda who?
Ice cream soda monsters won't get me.

Knock-knock.
   Who's there?
Icy.
   Icy who?
Icy you, do you see me?

Knock-knock.
   Who's there?
Ima.
   Ima who?
Ima ghost—BOO!

Knock-knock.
    Who's there?
I rest.
    I rest who?
I rest you in the name of the law!

Knock-knock.
    Who's there?
Irish.
    Irish who?
Irish all my dreams would come true.

Knock-knock.
    Who's there?
Isadora.
    Isadora who?
Isadora bit stuck?

Knock-knock.
    Who's there?
Iva.
    Iva who?
Iva piece of spinach stuck between my teeth.

Knock-knock.
    Who's there?
Ivan.
    Ivan who?
Ivan keeping my eye on you.

41

Knock-knock.
  Who's there?
Jackson.
  Jackson who?
Jackson is smarter than
John's son.

Knock-knock.
  Who's there?
Jamaica.
  Jamaica who?
Jamaica cake for my birthday?

Knock-knock.
    Who's there?
Jenny.
    Jenny who?
Jenny body live here besides you?

Knock-knock.
    Who's there?
Jewel.
    Jewel who?
Jewel remember me when
you open the door.

Knock-knock.
    Who's there?
Jess.
    Jess who?
Jess a minute, I forgot my
name.

Knock-knock.
    Who's there?
Jillian.
    Jillian who?
Jillian bucks I can
bungee jump off
the roof.

Knock-knock.
    Who's there?
Jilly.
    Jilly who?
Jilly out here, so let me in!

Knock-knock.
  Who's there?
Josette.
  Josette who?
Josette down and broke my chair!

Knock-knock.
  Who's there?
Juana.
  Juana who?
Juana come out and play?

Knock-knock.
  Who's there?
Juliet.
  Juliet who?
Juliet me in, right now!

Knock-knock.
  Who's there?
Jupiter.
  Jupiter who?
Jupiter fly in my soup?

Knock-knock.
  Who's there?
Justin.
  Justin who?
Justin credible, that's what you are.

Knock-knock.
  Who's there?
K. C.
  K. C. who?
K. C. doesn't come,
I'll lock the door.

Knock-knock.
  Who's there?
Kara.
  Kara who?
Kara lot about you. Do you
care about me?

Knock-knock.
  Who's there?
Kari.
  Kari who?
Kari me . . . my feet
are killing me.

Knock-knock.
   Who's there?
Karl.
   Karl who?
Karl break down . . . better fly.

Knock-knock.
   Who's there?
Ken.
   Ken who?
Ken you just answer the door?

Knock-knock.
   Who's there?
Karma.
   Karma who?
Karma long with me.

Knock-knock.
   Who's there?
Kenda.
   Kenda who?
Kenda dog come in too?

Knock-knock.
  Who's there?
Kent.
  Kent who?
Kent you tell? I'm
standing right here!

Knock-knock.
  Who's there?
Kiefer.
  Kiefer who?
Kiefer the door won't fit!

Knock-knock.
  Who's there?
Kilobytes.
  Kilobytes who?
Kilobytes if you pull Kilo's tail.

Knock-knock.
  Who's there?
Kimmy.
  Kimmy who?
Kimmy a hug, Honey.

Knock-knock.
  Who's there?
Kith and kin.
  Kith and kin who?
Kith you? I don't think I kin do that!

Knock-knock.
  Who's there?
Kurt N.
  Kurt N. who?
Kurt N. fell when I was taking a shower!

47

Knock-knock.
  Who's there?
Lauren.
  Lauren who?
Lauren order keep crime off
the streets.

Knock-knock.
  Who's there?
Leif.
  Leif who?
Leif the door unlocked
next time.

Knock-knock.
    Who's there?
Len.
    Len who?
Len me a dollar, will you?

Knock-knock.
    Who's there?
Les.
    Les who?
Les go for a swim!

Knock-knock.
    Who's there?
Letter.
    Letter who?
Letter in the house—she's getting all wet!

Knock-knock.
    Who's there?
Lettuce and peas.
    Lettuce and peas who?
Lettuce pray for world peas.

Knock-knock.
    Who's there?
Linus.
    Linus who?
Linus up so you can take attendance.

Knock-knock.
    Who's there?
Lion.
    Lion who?
Lion down again?

Knock-knock.
    Who's there?
Lisa.
    Lisa who?
Lisa you can do is let me in.

Knock-knock.
　Who's there?
Liver and bacon.
　Liver and bacon who?
　Liver alone! She's bacon me a cake!

Knock-knock.
　Who's there?
Lois.
　Lois who?
Lois down, high is up.

Knock-knock.
　Who's there?
Lotte.
　Lotte who?
Lotte people think
I'm crazy . . . do you?

Knock-knock.
　Who's there?
Louise.
　Louise who?
　Louise from France; eez you too?

Knock-knock.
　Who's there?
Luke.
　Luke who?
Luke, Ma!
No hands!

Knock-knock.
　Who's there?
Lyndon.
　Lyndon who?
Lyndon ear and I'll tell you.

50

Knock-knock.
 Who's there?
Maida.
  Maida who?
Maida force be with you.

Knock-knock.
 Who's there?
Marion.
  Marion who?
Marion someone you love
brings happiness.

Knock-knock.
  Who's there?
Marshall.
  Marshall who?
Marshall appear earlier than
Venus tonight.

Knock-knock.
  Who's there?
Max.
  Max who?
Max no difference to me.

Knock-knock.
  Who's there?
Maya.
  Maya who?
Maya best friend?

Knock-knock.
  Who's there?
Maybelle.
  Maybelle.
Maybelle doesn't ring either.

      Knock-knock.
        Who's there?
      Meat and pasta.
        Meat and pasta who?
      Meat me at home—it's way pasta your bedtime.

Knock-knock.
  Who's there?
Meg.
  Meg who?
Meg up your mind!

      Knock-knock.
        Who's there?
      Michelle.
        Michelle who?
      Michelle still has a snail in it.

      Knock-knock.
        Who's there?
      Midas.
        Midas who?
      Midas well let me in.

      Knock-knock.
        Who's there?
      Milkshakes.
        Milkshakes who?
      Milkshakes when cows dance.

53

Knock-knock.
    Who's there?
Minnie.
    Minnie who?
Minnie more jokes coming.

Knock-knock.
    Who's there?
Mischa.
    Mischa who?
Mischa when you were
gone—glad you're back!

Knock-knock.
    Who's there?
Mister.
    Mister who?
Mister bus, so
she had to walk.

Knock-knock.
    Who's there?
Mitosis.
    Mitosis who?
Mitosis cold . . . have you
seen my socks?

Knock-knock.
    Who's there?
Moose.
    Moose who?
Moose you be so nosy?

Knock-knock.
    Who's there?
Muffin.
    Muffin who?
Muffin wrong with me . . .
how about you?

Knock-knock.
  Who's there?
N.
  N who?
N exactly two seconds, I'm coming
N there!

Knock-knock.
  Who's there?
Nacho.
  Nacho who?
  Nacho fast, buster.

Knock-knock.
Who's there?
Necks.
Necks who?
Necks time, just open the door.

Knock-knock.
Who's there?
Neil.
Neil who?
Neil get scraped if you trip on your shoelaces.

Knock-knock.
Who's there?
Netta.
Netta who?
Netta butterfly, then set it free.

Knock-knock.
Who's there?
Nobel.
Nobel who?
Nobel, so I knocked.

Knock-knock.
Who's there?
No cents.
No cents who?
No cents talking to you.

Knock-knock.
  Who's there?
Nobody.
  Nobody who?
No body—I'm a ghost!

Knock-knock.
  Who's there?
Nonnie.
  Nonnie who?
Nonnie your business.

Knock-knock.
  Who's there?
Norway.
  Norway who?
Norway will I leave until
you open this door.

Knock-knock.
  Who's there?
Nutshell.
  Nutshell who?
Nutshell be my afternoon snack.

Knock-knock.
 Who's there?
Ocelot.
 Ocelot who?
Ocelot of questions, don't you?

Knock-knock.
 Who's there?
Oblong.
 Oblong who?
Oblong to a lot of clubs at school.

Knock-knock.
  Who's there?
Odessa.
  Odessa who?
Odessa good one!

Knock-knock.
  Who's there?
Odor.
  Odor who?
Odor me a
dessert, please.

Knock-knock.
  Who's there?
Offer.
  Offer who?
Offer got my key—let me in!

Knock-knock.
  Who's there?
Oleg.
  Oleg who?
Oleg of lamb makes a fine
Sunday dinner.

Knock-knock.
  Who's there?
Olga.
  Olga who?
Olga home if you don't open this door.

Knock-knock.
  Who's there?
Omega.
  Omega who?
Omega me some waffles, please.

Knock-knock.
  Who's there?
One shoe.
  One shoe who?
One shoe please open up!

Knock-knock.
  Who's there?
Ooze.
  Ooze who?
  Ooze in charge
  around here?

Knock-knock.
  Who's there?
Orange juice.
  Orange juice who?
Orange juice going to say you're sorry?

Knock-knock.
  Who's there?
Oscar.
  Oscar who?
Oscar silly question, get a silly
answer.

Knock-knock.
  Who's there?
Otis.
  Otis who?
Otis a sin to tell a lie.

Knock-knock.
  Who's there?
Owl.
  Owl who?
Owl aboard!

Knock-knock.
  Who's there?
Ozzie.
  Ozzie who?
Ozzie you later!

Knock-knock.
  Who's there?
Pablo.
  Pablo who?
Pablo your horn!

Knock-knock.
  Who's there?
Pansy.
  Pansy who?
Pansy scrubs in the sink; dishes
he puts in the dishwasher.

Knock-knock.
   Who's there?
Pasta.
   Pasta who?
Pasta salad, I'm starving!

Knock-knock.
   Who's there?
Pasture.
   Pasture who?
Pasture bedtime, isn't it?

Knock-knock.
   Who's there?
Patty O.
   Patty O. who?
Patty O. furniture is out by the pool.

Knock-knock.
   Who's there?
Peg.
   Peg who?
Peg your pardon . . . wrong door!

Knock-knock.
   Who's there?
Pigsty.
   Pigsty who?
Pigsty their tails up before they go out to play.

Knock-knock.
   Who's there?
Pisa.
   Pisa who?
Pisa pizza is my lunch.

Knock-knock.
  Who's there?
Pita.
  Pita who?
Pita Pan and Tinkerbell.

Knock-knock.
  Who's there?
Polly.
  Polly who?
Polly nation is what bees
do to flowers.

Knock-knock.
  Who's there?
Porky.
  Porky who?
Porky pines have sharp quills.

Knock-knock.
  Who's there?
Qs.
  Qs who?
Qs me . . . I'm going
to sneeze!

Knock-knock.
  Who's there?
Quark.
  Quark who?
Quark Kent is Superman's secret
identity.

Knock-knock.
  Who's there?
Quarter.
  Quarter who?
Quarter milk and a dozen
eggs, please.

Knock-knock.
  Who's there?
Quash.
  Quash who?
Quash up before you come
to the dinner table.

Knock-knock.
  Who's there?
Quiche.
  Quiche who?
Quiche me goodnight, Honeybun.

Knock-knock.
  Who's there?
Quiet Tina.
  Quiet Tina who?
Quiet Tina
courtroom!

Knock-knock.
  Who's there?
Quill.
  Quill who?
Quill you please leave me alone, Mr. Porcupine?

Knock-knock.
    Who's there?
Quilting bee.
    Quilting bee who?
Quilting bee a good hobby
for my grandma.

Knock-knock.
    Who's there?
Quiver.
    Quiver who?
Quiver back her
purse, you brute!

Knock-knock.
    Who's there?
Quota.
    Quota who?
Quota line from Shakespeare, and people will
think you're smart.

Knock-knock.
   Who's there?
Rabbit.
   Rabbit who?
Rabbit up carefully—it's a
birthday present.

Knock-knock.
   Who's there?
Radio.
   Radio who?
Radio not, here I come!

67

Knock-knock.
  Who's there?
Randy.
  Randy who?
Randy marathon—whew!

Knock-knock.
  Who's there?
Rhoda.
  Rhoda who?
Rhoda boat across the lake all by myself.

Knock-knock.
  Who's there?
Rhonda.
  Rhonda who?
Rhonda corner is where my best friend lives.

Knock-knock.
  Who's there?
Rita.
  Rita who?
Rita good book this week?

Knock-knock.
  Who's there?
Roland.
  Roland who?
Roland butter were my dinner.

Knock-knock.
Who's there?
Rollie.
Rollie who?
Rollie coaster rides scare me.

Knock-knock.
Who's there?
Rosa.
Rosa who?
Rosa corn grow in fields.

Knock-knock.
Who's there?
Rosanna.
Rosanna who?
Rosanna daffodil make a pretty bouquet.

Knock-knock.
   Who's there?
Rowan.
   Rowan who?
Rowan a boat is good exercise.

Knock-knock.
   Who's there?
Roxanne.
   Roxanne who?
Roxanne your head!

Knock-knock.
   Who's there?
Rufus.
   Rufus who?
Rufus on fire! Call 911!

Knock-knock.
   Who's there?
Russell.
   Russell who?
Russell do it if you pay him a dollar.

Knock-knock.
   Who's there?
Ryan.
   Ryan who?
Ryan oats are healthy grains.

Knock-knock.
   Who's there?
Sandal.
   Sandal who?
Sandal get in your trunks if
you sit on the beach.

Knock-knock.
   Who's there?
Sarah.
   Sarah who?
Sarah spider on my back?

Knock-knock.
    Who's there?
Satin.
    Satin who?
Satin your chair, and it broke.

Knock-knock.
    Who's there?
Saul Ted.
    Saul Ted who?
Saul Ted peanuts are healthy snacks.

Knock-knock.
    Who's there?
Sawyer.
    Sawyer who?
Sawyer underwear!

Knock-knock.
    Who's there?
Says.
    Says who?
Says me, that's who

Knock-knock.
    Who's there?
Scold.
    Scold who?
Scold enough to ice skate?

Knock-knock.
    Who's there?
Scott.
    Scott who?
Scott to be around here someplace.

Knock-knock.
    Who's there?
Seafood.
    Seafood who?
Seafood, smell food, then eat food.

Knock-knock.
    Who's there?
Sew.
    Sew who?
Sew clothes, yet so far.

Knock-knock.
    Who's there?
Seymour.
    Seymour who?
Seymour dolphins if you scare the sharks away first.

Knock-knock.
Who's there?
Senorita.
Senorita who?
Senorita taco. I'm eating a hot dog.

Knock-knock.
Who's there?
Sewer.
Sewer who?
Sewer you going to open the door, or what?

Knock-knock.
Who's there?
Shelby.
Shelby who?
Shelby coming over after she cleans her room.

Knock-knock.
Who's there?
Shore.
Shore who?
Shore is hot out here. Can I come in?

Knock-knock.
Who's there?
Sienna.
Sienna who?
Sienna good movies lately?

Knock-knock.
Who's there?
Sneeze.
Sneeze who?
Sneeze are dirty from kneeling in the garden

Knock-knock.
Who's there?
Spaghetti.
Spaghetti who?
Spaghetti, set, . . . go!

Knock-knock.
Who's there?
Stan.
Stan who?
Stan back, I'm going to burp!

Knock-knock.
Who's there?
Subway.
Subway who?
Subway more than a
ship weigh.

Knock-knock.
Who's there?
Summer.
Summer who?
Summer funny jokes, some aren't.

Knock-knock.
Who's there?
Summon.
Summon who?
Summon called me.
Was it you?

Knock-knock.
Who's there?
Sweden.
Sweden who?
Sweden my cereal with
sugar, please.

Knock-knock.
  Who's there?
Taco.
  Taco who?
Taco look at her!

Knock-knock.
  Who's there?
Tanks.
  Tanks who?
Tanks a lot!

Knock-knock.
  Who's there?
Tennis.
  Tennis who?
Tennis five plus five.

Knock-knock.
  Who's there?
Thatcher.
  Thatcher who?
Thatcher idea of a joke?

Knock-knock.
  Who's there?
There was an old woman.
  There was an old woman
  who?
Lived in a shoe.

Knock-knock.
  Who's there?
Thermos.
  Thermos who?
Thermos be a funnier
knock-knock than this one.

Knock-knock.
  Who's there?
Thumb.
  Thumb who?
Thumb body open this door!

Knock-knock.
  Who's there?
Thurston.
  Thurston who?
Thurston for some juice . . .
got any?

Knock-knock.
  Who's there?
Tim.
  Tim who?
Tim-burrr! Tree's falling!

77

Knock-knock.
  Who's there?
Tish.
  Tish who?
Tish who is good for blowing
your nose.

Knock-knock.
  Who's there?
Tommy.
  Tommy who?
Tommy aches . . .
must be something
I ate.

Knock-knock.
  Who's there?
Toucan.
  Toucan who?
Toucan eat more pizza than one can.

Knock-knock.
  Who's there?
Tucker.
  Tucker who?
Tucker in after she's said her prayers.

Knock-knock.
  Who's there?
Tuna and seashell.
  Tuna and seashell who?
Tuna piano, then seashell play her favorite song for you.

Knock-knock.
Who's there?
Turner.
Turner who?
Turner round so I can see your face.

Knock-knock.
Who's there?
Turnip.
Turnip who?
Turnip the radio—they're playing my favorite song!

Knock-knock.
Who's there?
Tutu.
Tutu who?
Tutu many people don't like ballet.

Knock-knock.
  Who's there?
Under.
  Under who?
Not under who, silly. Under where!

Knock-knock.
  Who's there?
U. R.
  U. R. who?
U. R. A. Q. T!

Knock-knock.
  Who's there?
User.
  User who?
User after Ts in the dictionary.

Knock-knock.
  Who's there?
Usher.
  Usher who?
Usher wish you'd let me in.

Knock-knock.
  Who's there?
Utah.
  Utah who?
Utah one in charge?

Knock-knock.
  Who's there?
U-turn.
  U-turn who?
U-turn the knob—that's how you open the door.

Knock-knock.
Who's there?
Van Gogh.
Van Gogh who?
Van Gogh slower than a Porsche.

Knock-knock.
  Who's there?
Veal.
  Veal who?
Veal be right back after a message from our sponsor.

Knock-knock.
  Who's there?
Vendor.
  Vendor who?
Vendor rain falls, my vindshield
vipers don't vork.

Knock-knock.
  Who's there?
Vincent.
  Vincent who?
Vincent me over—can I
come in?

Knock-knock.
  Who's there?
Vinnie.
  Vinnie who?
Vinnie you going to
answer the door?

Knock-knock.
  Who's there?
Vonna.
  Vonna who?
Vonna come over later?

83

Knock-knock.
    Who's there?
Waffle.
    Waffle who?
Waffle nice to meet you.

Knock-knock.
    Who's there?
Wagon.
    Wagon who?
Wagon its tail means your dog is happy.

Knock-knock.
   Who's there?
Waiter.
   Waiter who?
Waiter minute while I tie my shoes.

Knock-knock.
   Who's there?
Walter.
   Walter who?
Walter wall carpeting sure looks
good in my bedroom.

Knock-knock.
   Who's there?
Walleye.
   Walleye who?
Walleye declare!

Knock-knock.
   Who's there?
Warner.
   Warner who?
Warner not to come over—your
room's a mess!

Knock-knock.
   Who's there?
Warren.
   Warren who?
Warren Peace is a
classic Russian novel.

Knock-knock.
   Who's there?
Water.
   Water who?
Water you doing in my room?

Knock-knock.
  Who's there?
Waterfalls.
    Waterfalls who?
Waterfalls off the roof when it rains.

Knock-knock.
  Who's there?
Watson.
    Watson who?
Watson your schedule for tomorrow?

Knock-knock.
  Who's there?
Watts.
    Watts who?
Watts your point?

Knock-knock.
  Who's there?
Weed.
  Weed who?
Weed love to help you
eat that pizza.

Knock-knock.
  Who's there?
Weevil.
    Weevil who?
Weevil see you tomorrow.

Knock-knock.
  Who's there?
Weirdo.
    Weirdo who?
Weirdo you think you're going?

Knock-knock.
  Who's there?
Wheat.
    Wheat who?
Wheat better get going
or we'll be late.

Knock-knock.
  Who's there?
Wheel.
    Wheel who?
Wheel you please answer
the door!

Knock-knock.
  Who's there?
Wilda.
    Wilda who?
Wilda scary movie be on tonight?

Knock-knock.
  Who's there?
Wilfred.
  Wilfred who?
Wilfred clean my room if
I pay him?

Knock-knock.
  Who's there?
Willa.
  Willa who?
Willa dog bark if I knock
again?

Knock-knock.
  Who's there?
Wilma.
  Wilma who?
Wilma dinner be
ready soon?

Knock-knock.
  Who's there?
Winnie.
  Winnie who?
Winnie comes, I'm leaving!

Knock-knock.
  Who's there?
Woody.
  Woody who?
Woody let us play if we asked him nicely?

Knock-knock.
    Who's there?
X.
    X who?
X-tremely pleased to meet you!

Knock-knock.
    Who's there?
X. C.
    X. C. who?
X. C. –lent!

    Knock-knock.
      Who's there?
    X. R.
      X. R. who?
    X. R. my favorite breakfast food.

Knock-knock.
  Who's there?
X. Q.
    X. Q. who?
X. Qs me.

Knock-knock.
  Who's there?
Xylene.
    Xylene who?
Xylene over to paint my toenails.

Knock-knock.
  Who's there?
Xyster.
    Xyster who?
Xyster is a lot nicer than my brother.

Knock-knock.
  Who's there?
Y. O. Y.
  Y. O. Y. who?
Y. O. Y. did you lock this
door?

Knock-knock.
  Who's there?
Yachts.
  Yachts who?
Yachts of luck.

GOOD FORTUNE

Knock-knock.
Who's there?
Yam.
Yam who?
Yam what I yam and that's all that I yam.

Knock-knock.
Who's there?
Yelp.
Yelp who?
Yelp me! I can't
get in the house!

Knock-knock.
Who's there?
Yoda, yoda, lady.
Yoda, yoda, lady who?
Hey, I didn't know you could yodel!

Knock-knock.
Who's there?
Your pencil.
Your pencil who?
Your pencil fall down if you
don't wear a belt.

Knock-knock.
Who's there?
Yugo.
Yugo who?
Yugo first, I'll follow.

Knock-knock.
  Who's there?
Zaire.
  Zaire who?
Zaire is higher on ze head
zan on ze mouth.

Knock-knock.
  Who's there?
Zat.
  Zat who?
Zat your final answer?

Knock-knock.
  Who's there?
Zinc.
  Zinc who?
Zinc in the kitchen is full of dirty dishes.

Knock-knock.
  Who's there?
Zing.
  Zing who?
Zing a zong of zixpence.

Knock-knock.
  Who's there?
Zipper.
  Zipper who?
Zipper dee-doo-dah.

Knock-knock.
  Who's there?
Zits.
  Zits who?
Zits got to be
the place.

Knock-knock.
  Who's there?
Zizi.
  Zizi who?
Zizi once you get the
hang of it.

Knock-knock.
  Who's there?
Zoey.
  Zoey who?
Zoey now are coming to the end of this book.

Knock-knock.
   Who's there?
Zombies.
   Zombies who?
Zombies make honey; some bees just buzz around.

Knock-knock.
   Who's there?
Zubin.
   Zubin who?
Zubin eating garlic
again?

Knock-knock.
   Who's there?
Zori.
   Zori who?
Zori to tell you—you zpilled
zoda on your zuit.

Knock-knock.
   Who's there?
Zuni.
   Zuni who?
Zuni or later, this book
has to end.

Knock-knock.
   Who's there?
Zygote.
   Zygote who?
Zygote maybe one more joke to tell.

Knock-knock.
   Who's there?
Zyme.
   Zyme who?
Zyme all done—Zee ya!

Index